HOW TO VALUE A BUSINESS

An Incredibly Accurate and Simple Way to Confidently Value a Business

DEDICATION

I dedicate this little book to the little woman behind the great man who wrote it. In all seriousness my wife Rona, a CPA, provided the inspiration to have me put pen to paper (actually keyboard to computer), to document what I have been exposing to friends and clients through the years.

ACKNOWLEDGMENTS

No one in particular

The fact is that there is very little written on this subject. When I approached a number of people who I felt should be knowledgeable on this subject, they all went into a lengthy dissertation. It was like asking someone what time it was and being told how a watch works. Well, this book simply tells you what time it is!

Copyright © 1996 Frank M. Singer, BSME, MBA

All rights reserved. No part of this book may be used or reproduced in any manner whatsoever without the written permission of the Publisher.

Printed in the United States of America.

For information address
Frank M. Singer
3552 Venture Drive
Huntington Beach, CA 92649
fsinger@socal.rr.com
www.valueabusiness.com

Library of Congress Catalog Card Number 99-62347

Singer, Frank M.
How to Value a Business

ISBN 0-9671267-0-3

First Edition - 1999
Second Edition - 2006
Third Edition - 2010

Book Designed by Loretta Hwong at GO Brand Engineering
www.thinkgo.com

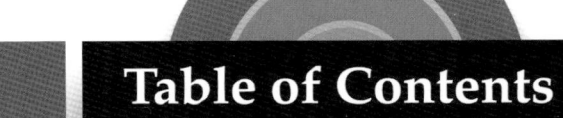

Table of Contents

Chapter	Title	Page
	Preface	1
1	Types of Valuations	4
2	Valuing the Ongoing Business	7
3	Strategic Valuations	17
4	Other Considerations	19
5	Anecdotes	24
	Epilogue	28

BY FRANK M. SINGER

Preface

I have found that the one single thing that people have trouble with is placing a value on a business. Now, for the purpose of defining a business I will include anything that generates revenue for the purpose of creating a profit. Not included of course, would be a non-profit business or organization like a charity. If a non-profit business were put up for sale, God only would know how to value it (and maybe He should, especially if it's a charity).

When I say *anything* that is exactly what I mean. I don't care if the business is large or small, a manufacturer, a service provider like an accounting or law office, real estate holdings, a doctor's office, a start up business that does not as yet have any revenue, or an old line mature business. Anything that generates (or should) a profit. This book (if you call it that) will explain how to value any of these businesses and many more not even mentioned above.

I am writing this primer (because that is all it is) because I find it appalling how little people know about placing a value on their business, or placing a value on a business they want to acquire. My business school training spent virtually no time whatsoever on valuing a business. I have searched libraries and book stores and

found virtually nothing of value. There are companies, of course that will charge you an arm and a leg (or some other body part) to develop a value for your business. The IRS is only too happy to place a value for your business. CPA's often struggle on placing a value on a business. Bankers are the worst at placing and understanding the value of a business. Yet, it is a surprisingly simple exercise, as the reader will quickly learn when he or she reads this short book.

Don't be discouraged or mislead by the brevity of this "book". I could have actually put the essentials down one just one page as you will see. I have added some extra chapters to satisfy skeptics and answer a few questions before they are asked. I would have loved to make this booklet much thicker to impress the reader (I even thought of using thicker paper or a larger font). The fact of the matter, however, is that valuing a business is a very simple matter as the reader will see in the following few chapters. It should not take more than thirty to sixty minutes to get through and fully understand this primer and become an expert in valuing a business. The "fog" index of what you are about to read is very low.

After going through this primer and comprehending the simple techniques described herein, there is no question in my mind that the reader will agree that they are getting their money's worth. I have exposed this approach to countless business professionals and academics. All

have been amazed by both the accuracy and brevity as well as the simplicity of the techniques described herein. So far no one has challenged my approach.

Just one more note. I am not that arrogant to imply that the techniques described herein are the one and only ways to place a value on a business (I do however at times come across as arrogant, sorry, get over it). At the very least they are a reality check. The reader is certainly free (actually it isn't free) to engage an expert to make a more detailed analysis as to a business' worth.

So please read on. If you feel you are not being educated you will at least be entertained.

Chapter 1

Types of Value

Businesses have basically **three** values. This might be an oversimplification but this whole book or primer uses the "KISS" approach, Keep It Stupidly Simple (or is it Keep It Simple, Stupid?).

To waste space I could use one chapter of this book for each of the value types, but that would go against the grain of the "KISS" approach.

Value #1: **Liquidation Value**

This is the value of a business that most likely is going out of business. Here the value might be close to the Book Value shown on the company's Balance Sheet. If the business is going to liquidate, it could be an orderly liquidation or a fire sale liquidation. In either case the number will be something related to the Book Value of the business. This type of valuation is not the subject matter of this book.

Value # 2: **Stock Value**

For a public company or a company going public in an

Initial Public Offering (IPO), God only knows how to value this situation. Of course the underwriters, many of whom consider themselves gods, will quickly come up with a value. This is an art not a science, and I would not even begin to speculate on how companies going public get valued. There seems to be no sense or logic in how this happens. My guess is that IPOs go by the "greater fool" theory. And that theory, as many of you know, is that when a fool buys into an IPO the fool hopes that there is a greater fool to take him or her out.

There is also a strategy involving valuation when a start-up seeks second and subsequent rounds of financing. This has to do with various classes of stock and revolves around per share pricing, warrants, and a host of other schemes and can get very complex. For this you will need a very clever transaction attorney. The total value of the company however, before there is a public price, can still be ascertained using the techniques described in this book. Again, this primer on valuing a business does not purport to explain how per share pricing is done. It does, however guide you through the first valuation you will need so you will know how much of your company you will have to give away to get your initial round of financing.

Value #3: **Ongoing Business Value**

We finally get to what all of you have been waiting for.

The following chapters will very clearly show the reader how to value a business no matter what type of business it is, its size, or stage of maturity. I suppose there is an exception which would be the not-for-profit business, such as charitable organizations. These types of businesses do have a value. A brief explanation in the last chapter will at least give an approach to valuing this kind of business or organization.

Chapter 2

Valuing the Ongoing Business

This chapter is and this page is really the essence of this book. Please don't be mislead by the simple elegance of **The Formula**. It works and soon you will be an expert in valuing your own or someone else's business. It should only take a few minutes to calculate. It isn't brain surgery. **The Formula** is:

Value = NAT x P x PVM x 8

Where:

- **NAT** = Net after Tax income at some time in the future
- **P** = the Probability that the NAT will be achieved
- **PVM** = the present value of future money
- **8** = 8 (explained more fully on the next page)

To make this equation work, NAT, from the P & L statement, needs to be recast or normalized. Normalizing means to make any adjustments up or down to account for what should or should not normally be in your profit

and loss statement. For example the company yacht should be taken out (increases NAT), or if you are not paying yourself a "normal" salary, add the amount that you should normally be paid (decreases NAT), etc.

A word here on NAT. Some would argue that EBIT (earnings before interest and tax), or more specifically earnings, should not include interest. This is not a realistic approach and actually would not change the numbers all that much. First, it isn't realistic because most businesses use bank debt or some other form of debt to finance working capital. Debt is normal. Secondly, eliminating interest from earnings would increase earnings (NAT) thus giving a higher valuation. However if interest is removed then bank debt should also be removed. In other words, the buyer would not assume bank debt if interest were not used to determine earnings. The reader will find that the overall valuation of the business, by eliminating interest, would closely be offset by the bank debt. *The buyer would pay more for the business but not assume the bank debt.* It all works out about the same.

That's it. Isn't that the model of simplicity? A little further explanation is in order. First of all you will note that the Balance Sheet does not come into the equation. The reason for this is that a company is only worth as a function of what it can earn. Certainly an asset rich company will have some effect on price because the buyer can leverage the assets for borrowing purposes, but, by and large, earnings is what it is all about because we all live

by return on investment. Of course if the assets make the company's net worth higher than its value as derived herein, liquidation might make a more viable alternative.

There is also the distinction of a financial versus a strategic acquisition. Certainly a strategic acquisition would make a company more valuable. Strategic values will be addressed in the next chapter. However the fundamental formula does not change. Let's look at a few examples.

Example A

A small manufacturer has been running along at a sales level of $5 million and has an after tax profit of $400,000. His wife works as his bookkeeper and he only pays her a salary of $12,000. First we have to normalize earnings. If the wife would stay on at $12,000 there would be no adjustment. If, however after the sale, the new buyer would have to replace her with a $35,000 bookkeeper, earnings would have to be adjusted downward. The economy looks pretty stable so future earnings are fairly predictable with few surprises. The owner has a vacation cabin on the company books. The cost of maintaining the cabin should be removed which would increase NAT. So, let's say normalized earnings would bring NAT to $450,000 by the end of next year calculated as follows:

> Reported after tax profit $400,000
> Add normal bookkeeper salary   (23,000)
> Remove cabin maintenance   28,000

Two year business increase	45,000
Next year NAT	$450,000

Let's look at "P". This is the probability that the manufacturer will be able to generate a NAT of $450,000 two years hence. "P" in this case is not that difficult to estimate. After all it can't be less than "0" or greater than "1". I would put a 90% probability that the NAT of $450,000 will be achieved in year two. This makes P = .9. PVM is simply the present value of future money. If the cost of money is 10% then a dollar one year from now is only worth $.91 today. A dollar two years from now is only worth $.83 today and so on. Use the table below for discounting future money at a cost of money of 10%.

PVM Discount Factor	Year
.91	1
.83	2
.75	3
.68	4
.62	5

For this example since we are looking at year 2 we will use a PVM = .83, so for Example A.

PV = $450,000 x .9 x .83 x 8 = $2,689,200

One should not take this valuation to be cast in concrete.

BY FRANK M. SINGER

A leeway of plus or minus 10% would certainly be reasonable.

Now the reader most likely wants to know what the "8" stands for. This will give a generally accepted before tax return of investment of 20% to 25% or an after tax return of 10% to 15%. To clarify let's look at it this way.

Multiplying by eight gives a return of $1 per year (after taxes) for every $8 invested. So if $1,000 is invested one would expect to get back $125 per year (8 x 125 = 1,000) after taxes. That is a return of 12.5% after taxes or 20% to 25% before taxes depending on your tax bracket. If you want a higher return use a lower multiplier. The following multipliers give the after tax returns on your investment:

Multiplier	After Tax ROI
6	16.7%
7	14.3%
8	**12.5%**
9	11.1%
10	10.0%

I have found through the years that "8" makes a good multiplier providing a reasonable ROI. I could have used a "10", but that would make it too easy to calculate (and results in a lower ROI), besides "8" makes for more interesting conversation.

HOW TO VALUE A BUSINESS

Let's look at another example.

Example B

An entrepreneur presents a business plan for a new software product. The idea looks good and the management team looks like they have had applicable experience. There is no revenue for the first year, but in a few years the famous "hockey stick" shows incredible revenue and profits.

The plan asks for the standard $1 million from investors for which it is willing to give up 25% of the company.

Is this a good deal? The plan reveals the following:

		(000's)			
Item	Year 1	Year 2	Year 3	Year 4	Year 5
Sales	$25	$300	$1,500	$3,000	$6,000
NAT	($200)	($100)	$100	$300	$750

In this case due diligence shows that the plan is sound and that the software will eventually have wide applications. I would give the probability that the $750,000 after tax profit in year five can be achieved at 5% to 10% (however, I usually give a green start up a probability of 3% to 5%).

The valuation would therefore be:

$$PV = \$750{,}000 \times .075 \times .62 \times 8 = \$279{,}000$$

In this case it would be hard for the group to raise $1,000,000 for 25% of a company that only has a present value of $279,000. In the formula, the .075 represents a generous 7.5% chance that the entity will make it (the average of 5% and 10%). The .62 represents the present value of a dollar five years hence. In other words, 62¢ invested at 10% would grow to about a dollar in five years.

You might ask "suppose I use a different year to make the valuation, say year three". Well let's see what that yields. The valuation for year three would be:

$$PV = \$100{,}000 \times .45 \times .75 \times 8 = \$270{,}000$$

As the reader can see, it does not make that much difference which year is used (both valuations would round off to $275,000). For year three a 45% probability was used because it would be more realistic (a higher probability) to make a $100,000 NAT in year three than a $750,000 NAT in year five. Obviously the formula is largely influenced by the probability used, but after analyzing a business plan it will be almost second nature to pick a number that in itself is realistic. Note that the PVM discount factor for year three is .75.

HOW TO VALUE A BUSINESS

In this example the business is obviously not worth pursuing. Investing $1,000,000 for 25% of a business that only expects to make a few hundred thousand dollars of profit in a few years is just not prudent. Now if the company had a product that was a slam dunk and there was a high degree of certainty that revenue and profit projections would be met, then it could be worth more, but still not enough for a $1 million investment. I would advise such a company to develop higher revenue and profit projections and/or struggle along and test the market so that there would be a higher probability that down stream projections will be more achievable.

PRE-MONEY VALUATIONS

At this point I feel I should make a point about "pre-money" valuations. For a start-up company an investor often talks about pre or post money valuations. What the investor means by these terms is the value of a business before and after an investment has been made. Say the formula for a new investment shows that the business is worth $3,000,000 and an investment of $1,000,000 is being sought. The investor would say that the pre-money valuation is $3,000,000 and after his investment the entity would be worth $4,000,000. This sounds like a sound argument, but it is WRONG!

Now I am sure the entire investment community will take issue with me on this. I have no argument that a start-up business will be worth more *after* an investment. Where I take issue is how the after-investment value of the entity is determined. It is very simple to just add the value of the investment to the pre-money value. However, a more accurate method of determining the post-money valuation is by assessing the new risk, or probability of attaining the profit objectives. By adding money to the new business the risk of failure goes down and consequently "P" in the formula goes up. If the "P" (probability) goes up, so does the valuation. In many cases the post-money valuation would be considerably higher than by just adding the new investment to the "pre-money" valuation.

Incidentally, pre-money and post-money valuations only apply to start-ups. In buying or selling an ongoing business there is no such thing as pre-money or post-money considerations.

Chapter 3

Strategic Valuations

There is only one further refinement regarding the valuation of a business. The previous chapter addressed valuation from a purely financial outlook. In many cases a business will have a strategic value to the acquirer. A company might want to make an acquisition to gain market share, improve its own technology, get rid of competition, or a host of other reasons. In such a case the increase in value of the acquiring company that would occur as a result of the acquisition could arguably be added to the value of the business being acquired. Let's look at an example.

The business being acquired is mature and expected to grow 5% with a high degree (90%) of probability. Next year it expects to net $750,000 after taxes. A financial valuation would then be:

$$PV = \$750{,}000 \times .9 \times .91 \times 8 = \$4{,}914{,}000$$

The acquiring company *without* the acquisition expects to have an after tax profit next year of $5,000,000. With the acquisition the acquiring company expects to increase their own after tax profit in year two after the acquisition by $1,500,000 with a 75% probability. The question now is, "How much more is the company to be acquired strategically worth?" The calculation is really very simple.

    Increased Value of Acquirer
       = $1,500,000 x .75 x .83 x 8 = $7,470,000

This then would make the company being acquired worth $4,914,000 + $7,470,000 or $12,384,000. That's correct, it would be worth almost three times more than in a purely financial acquisition. This shows the importance of selling a business in a strategic transaction. I am sure many readers have wondered why some companies have fetched such high prices. A savvy seller or buyer knows the value of strategic transactions. Everybody really wins.

Someone once asked me to make an investment because it was the "right thing" to do. I reflected and responded that I spend money for only two reasons: (1) To make more money, and (2) To buy something that makes me feel good. So far, I have not found a third reason to spend money. This book lets you make a more analytical evaluation of (1). As far as (2) is concerned that is entirely up to the reader. That is a subject I could write a real book about, but it would take me too long, and I would rather buy something I like instead.

Chapter 4

Other Considerations

Suppose you are looking at a company that has been losing money. How much is it worth? The first question you have to ask yourself is "Can this company be turned around?" If you think you can turn it around with a fair or high degree of probability, you can use those probabilities in the basic valuation formula.

If you don't think the company can be turned around, maybe the sellers should give you money to take it off their hands. Don't laugh, it has been done. The Valuation Formula would not work, but you can look at it in the following way.

Here is an example:

The Ajax Company has been losing $150,000 per year for the past year and expects to lose that much for at least the next year. You think with a high degree of certainty (80%), that you can generate an after tax profit of $100,000 in year two and a certainty of 50% that you can generate an after tax $300,000 profit in year three. This is after investing $300,000 for new equipment and upgrad-

ing management. The Book Value of the company is $300,000. How much is this business worth to you?

If you expect to keep the company going it will take at least the $150,000 projected loss to keep it solvent for the coming year. Added to that would be what you felt it would take to turn it around. That could be adding new management and equipment. Since the Book Value is relatively high, the company does have some value. In fact, any time that the Book Value is higher than the value derived from the Valuation Formula one must take that into consideration because liquidation is always an option. An orderly liquidation appraisal might be in order under these circumstances.

Anyway, back to the example. One must analyze what it will take to turn the company around and how long it would take. Using the above assumptions, we come up with the following:

$$PV = \$100{,}000 \times .8 \times .83 \times 8 = \$531{,}200 \text{ (Valuation after year two)}$$

$$PV = \$300{,}000 \times .5 \times .75 \times 8 = \$900{,}000 \text{ (Valuation after year three)}$$

The question now is which valuation to use. A strong argument could be made for either. Not that they are that far apart. Note that a lower probability is used for year three (50%) because it is further away and therefore harder to estimate. A fair valuation would be to average the two numbers and use around $700,000 for the valuation. From this we should deduct the $150,000 loss for the first year and the $300,000 for new equipment and management. A fair price would then be:

$$\$700{,}000 - \$150{,}000 - \$300{,}000 = \$250{,}000$$

This is not much different than the Book or Salvage Value, so it is probably a realistic and fair valuation. The seller might think differently (they always do), but from your standpoint you now have a good feel and basis to make an informed decision based on various valuations.

There are many variations, but they all come down to *return on investment*. The owner of a losing business has to make the choice of pouring more money into the business, selling it or liquidating it. If the owner decides to "get out", and wants to protect employees, he might take a lower sell price rather than liquidating the business. This, and countless other considerations, is beyond the scope of this Primer, The reader however should take comfort in knowing that over 90% of the businesses being evaluated will be straight forward and not require "other considerations".

NOT-FOR-PROFIT ORGANIZATIONS

As promised in the Preface, I will try to lay out a strategy

BY FRANK M. SINGER

for placing a value on a not-for-profit business or organization. There are a number of different types of not-for-profit businesses. There are social clubs, religious organizations, charitable organizations, utilities and so on. Other than a larger charitable organization (like the Red Cross), not-for-profit businesses are generally not for sale and their value is mostly intrinsic. However, an organization such as the Red Cross does have value. Since this type of organization does not show a profit (they do show surpluses and deficits on their books) one would have to derive a profit using other means. The most logical basis would be total revenue. An old rule of thumb was that a company generating a normal or decent profit is worth what its sales are. In other words, if a non-profit organization generated $100 million in revenue it is worth $100 million.

While the above is an over simplification it does give the reader a token idea on valuing these types of organizations. The purpose of this primer is really to help the reader value traditional for-profit businesses. I believe I have done that. I only bring up these other types of organizations (businesses) so that someone can't come back to me and say I didn't help them place a value on the Saint Mary's Home for Blind Rabbis and ask for their money back.

REAL ESTATE

Just a word on the value of income producing real estate.

Real Estate has a value not necessarily only related to the net income one derives from tenants. Real property can be appraised by adding land value to the cost of construction. Sometimes a landlord might rent his property at a loss expecting the property to increase in value. So just looking at "NAT" income might not give the true value of the property. One would have to factor in any change in value the property might have in the long term and add (or subtract) this to a multiple of earnings. In other words, one can use The Formula described in Chapter 2 and add the result to any change in property value one might expect at some time in the future. It is beyond the scope of this book to tackle real estate values. One caveat however. In the long run it still boils down to *return on investment*. The landlord must still figure on obtaining a reasonable return on his or her investment by adjusting rents in concert with any change in the value the landlord expects on the property itself. In some cases a landowner might just sit on the property without leasing it out if the owner felt there was going to be a dramatic increase in its worth in the foreseeable future. It still boils down to annualized *return on investment*.

Chapter 5

Anecdotes

This chapter describes a few anecdotes that should reinforce the utility of the techniques described in this booklet. The following stories are true and only the names and places have been changed to protect the innocent (me).

Anecdote 1

A friend of mine, a chiropractor, was retiring and wanted to sell his practice. He told me he wanted $75,000 and asked me what I thought. After a few minutes of asking him some questions, I told him his practice was worth double what he was asking for. He took my advice and listed his practice with a broker for $150,000 and got an offer for that amount within ten days. My friend was angry with me because he thought the price I gave him was too low because it sold so fast. We are still sort of friends.

Anecdote 2

A client of mine wanted to acquire a Canadian division of of a Fortune 100 company. They hired a prominent Wall

Street investment banker to come up with a valuation. At the same time I studied the books of the division to be acquired. In less than an hour I came up with a number and wrote it on a piece of paper and gave it to my client. I told him not to look at the number until he got the report from the investment banker. After three months and $35,000, the investment banker delivered a proposal that looked like the Manhattan phone book. They came up with a valuation of $20,000,000 plus or minus 5% or $1,000,000. My number was $23,500,000. But the story gets better.

My client submitted a sealed bid of $22,000,000 for the Canadian division. Our competitor won with a bid of $23,500,000. To this day I think my client thinks I leaked my number to his competitor (I didn't).

Anecdote 3

A neighbor was in a partnership that owned over 1,000 rental units in Southern California. He wanted to sell his interest to his partners, but no one had any idea of what the partnership was worth. They had been partners for over twenty years. My neighbor came to me for help in valuing the partnership. We spent less than one hour going over the partnership financials trying to normalize them and I finally came up with a valuation.

Now, real estate is another animal. A piece of real estate property does have a value aside from what it can earn in the near future. This might be true due to market conditions that might indicate that a certain piece of property might go up or down in value. One might accept lower immediate earnings from real property with the expectation that it will go up in value. Here again, however, return on investment is the underlying principal under which we operate. Adam West's "Economic Man" still describes us pretty well. Anyway, I digress.

All the partners agreed to my number because it was right in the middle of what my neighbor thought the business was worth and what his partners thought it was worth. There were other considerations, which complicated the valuation, having to do with the business such as administration, maintenance, reserves, and so forth, each having a P & L impact. There was also the question of what the value of the property would be if it were sold. This was solved by letting my neighbor share in an increase in value of any property sold within five years (there are many ways to skin a cat…sorry Fluffy).

My approach at least gave credibility to the numbers that the partners were kicking around because it focused on ROI (return on investment). To this day my neighbor is still impressed over how I could come up with a number so fast that they had been agonizing over for so many months. Of course both sides were a bit upset because they didn't get all they wanted, but I have always said that a good negotiation is when both sides feel equally screwed. This was a good negotiation.

There are many more anecdotes, but by now the reader should get the idea that there is some credibility to my approach. I, of course, also use these techniques in evaluating start up businesses. It seems entrepreneurs have a habit of placing quite excessive values on their businesses. I have only used the foregoing anecdotes to show the breath of businesses that can use and one can apply my techniques.

Epilogue

OK, for those who are still looking for page 13, there is no page 13 because in this great country of ours superstitious people don't like that number. Look at most buildings. There is no thirteenth floor! I for one like the number thirteen because I was not only born on the 13th, but on Friday the 13th. So to satisfy the masses and not spook anyone I have eliminated page 13. Furthermore, I get paid by the page and the publisher only looks at the number on the last page (the European version of this book will have a page 13 so as not to drive them crazy).

This book (primer) can easily contain many more pages, but if I added any more I would start making things up. The Formula contained in this primer works, regardless of the size and type of for profit businesses or even their stage of development. The reason for this is quite simple: investors want to make a fair return on their investment commensurate with the risk. The range of return investors generally seek is usually 20% to 30% before taxes or 10% to 15% after taxes. It's just that simple.

As I mentioned in the Preface, the techniques described herein are not the final word in valuing a business, but at the very least they are a quick (and not so dirty) reality check.

Final Thought

If we postulate that:

    Knowledge = Power and

    Time = Money

And we substitute (equate) Power and Time in the familiar Power Equation

    Power = Work/Time

we come up with:

    Money = Work/Knowledge

From this we learn that as Knowledge increases, Money approaches zero regardless of how much Work we do. So, hopefully you will not have gained too much knowledge from this book.

OK, One More "Final" Thought

Before this Epilogue becomes another Chapter I'll try to keep this last thought short. The other day I came across a new term "EBIDA". It seems that there are endless ways to analyze things to death. I always like to express my ignorance (how else do we learn?) by asking my learned friend as to what that meant. He proudly said

BY FRANK M. SINGER

"earnings before interest, depreciation, and amortization". I wondered what that had to do with the price of eggs in China, but held my thoughts to myself. After getting back to my office I finally realized what "EBIDA" really means (I later found some people use EBITDA to exclude taxes). It sort of represents *cash flow* without debt. I say "sort of" because Interest should be in the equation because it does effect cash flow. Well, cash flow is important but it does not necessarily relate to valuation. Cash flow is an *operational* consideration. Actually a banker's (and the mafia's) mentality has to do with "how will my client pay back my loan?" The value of the business is incidental to the banker. Cash flow is what is important and the banker usually does not take out taxes because he needs the business to stay solvent so the loan gets paid back.

I ran into someone recently who used EBITDA for valuation. He used this formula:

$$\text{Valuation} = 6 \times \text{EBITDA} - 3 \times \text{Debt}$$

He was surprised to come up with a similar valuation as I did using my formula. If that's the case why bother with EBITDA? He came to the same conclusion. My bottom line take is that EBITDA is useless and confuses everyone. It has no practical purpose that I can determine. Actually I have no idea what it signifies. I'll give anyone a prize who can tell me.

Cash flow is actually great when you are going out of business. You are selling your inventory and assets and not buying anything. Likewise when business is growing, cash flow is dismal. Again, cash flow is an operational thing. I am sure certain businesses might have more value if they generate a lot of cash, but the bottom line is still ROI. That is why we make investments. We want to know the return we can expect after making the investment. It's that simple, so The Formula in Chapter 2 still stands undefeated:

$$\text{Valuation} = \text{NAT} \times \text{P} \times \text{PVM} \times 8$$

Gertrude Stein said, "A rose is a rose is a rose, etc" President Bush (or was it that lizard looking guy?) said, "It's the economy stupid". Well I say "its Return on Investment, Stupid. Return on Investment, Stupid. Return of Investment, Stupid. etc".

Now don't you think you got your money's worth when you purchased this book? By applying "The Formula" to the price of this book you should easily come up with a value one hundred times more than what you paid.

Notes:

Notes: